A Couple
Of Words

Mavioglu, H, I,
The Journey of the Soul
ISBN: 0-595-30556-3

A Couple Of Words

Book I

H. I. Mavioglu

iUniverse, Inc.
New York Lincoln Shanghai

A Couple Of Words
Book I

Copyright © 2005 by Hilmi Mavioglu

All rights reserved. No part of this book may be used or reproduced by any means, graphic, electronic, or mechanical, including photocopying, recording, taping or by any information storage retrieval system without the written permission of the publisher except in the case of brief quotations embodied in critical articles and reviews.

iUniverse books may be ordered through booksellers or by contacting:

iUniverse
2021 Pine Lake Road, Suite 100
Lincoln, NE 68512
www.iuniverse.com
1-800-Authors (1-800-288-4677)

Cover design
By Malcom McKisson
"Pages at Opera House"

ISBN: 0-595-34721-5

Printed in the United States of America

Thread of poetry that passes through from heart
To heart is spun with words of many colors.

Acknowledgement

These poems came to me at their chosen eternal moment.
I celebrated their birth with the following kindred spirits:
Susan and Don Barnes, N.H.I. Basho, Andrea Cook, Rebecca Dean, Grace R. Long, Joyce, Nesli and Kurt Mavioglu, Richard Meister Jr., Laura Moyers, Pat Pfeiffer, Christa Richardson and Larry Treffry.

Table of Contents

State of Nothingness 1

To Love for Love's Sake 2

Life Chooses its Own Channel 3

The Answers Are up in the Air 4

One More Open Door 6

World of Dreams 7

Naked Nature 8

The Gift 9

Masked Blessings 11

Imperceptible Time 13

Identity 14

Retiring on the Job 18

Is There a Defect in the Design? 19

Straight Lines Curve 20

Crimson Poppy 21

The Rose and the Weed 26

Emmanuel 27

Shades of Change 36

Beauty Remembered 37

Let's Bless Them All 43

A Couple Of Words

Man Would Not Begin if he Were Afraid of the End 44
Desecration of Dartford Peak 46
    I.   *A Sudden Change* *47*
    II.   *One Spark Can Kindle Many Flame* *50*
    III.   *We Choose What Is Sacred for Us* *51*
    IV.   *River Runs Downward but Returns Upward* *53*
    V.   *Zeke's Memories Reshape What Is Shapeless* *57*
    VI.   *The Bigger the Project, the Larger the Profit* *63*
    VII. *Is There Anybody Who Cares?* *64*
    VIII. *Can We Have Progress Without its Consequences?* *67*
    IX.   *We Do Things Differently Since We Are More Civilized* *68*
    X.   *Who Is to Blame?* *69*
    XI.   *Impermanence* *73*
    XII. *Walking Away From a Lost Shrine* *76*

State of Nothingness

After molting my false feathers, I sank
But leveled off at level land of frank
Nothingness. Some rise spiraling upward,
Yet time levels all to an even rank.

To Love for Love's Sake

As the lovers slumber, love stays awake.
When I sense that love is unlimited,
I begin to learn to love for love's sake.

In the game of love, whole heart is at stake.
As I chase, I sense that I'm being led.
As the lovers slumber, love stays awake.

The love's edge sears, but its center will slake.
It's not love's fire, but its freeze that I dread,
And I try to learn to love for love's sake.

The heart grows hale with each song or heartache.
For love it's the heart that counts not the head.
As the lovers slumber, love stays awake.

To gain extra time, I rose by daybreak.
Who can hoard time? As always it had fled,
But by then, I'd time to love for love's sake.

Your gifts, a smile and a kiss by the lake,
Hold us together like a pure gold thread.
As the lovers slumber, love stays awake.
I have learnt by heart to love for love's sake.

Life Chooses its Own Channel

He said, "Plan and prime your life." And I planned.
She said, "Have visions and dreams." And I dreamt.
I tried to tame life to mind my command.
It must have been a fanciful attempt.

Now my dreams are neither alive nor dead.
My life meanders in its chosen bed.

The Answers Are up in the Air

Who piled up nonexistence, setting it on fire
To fashion this universe? Who skillfully ground
Its parts to fit? Who set the pressure of the air
And freed it to flow? Who gave phases to the water?
Who hollowed out the nil to turn it into space?
Who channeled nurturing things to run into life?

We stare at stars through the narrow window of life,
And what we perceive as light is nothing but fire.
It's measured by years; yet there's too short of a space
Between our lending and departure from this ground.
Before diving, one may choose to fathom the water;
Fathomless is the future and up in the air.

Heedlessly hoarding for the future gives an air
Of security. Will we ever learn that life
Blossoms in a state of balance? Some extra water
Drowns, a gentle breeze rekindles embers of fire
And drives it to burn everything down to the ground
While a wildfire suffocates in an airless space.

Yet people deserve to have their personal space
To form their own microcosms, to have an air
Of selfhood, a sanctuary to go to ground
To dream and to wait for their dreams to come to life.
For the folk hardship is a shirt of fire,
But for the winners dark clouds are the source of water.

Shall I hound after every novelty to water
Down the sap of life and crowd my living space?
Shall I slave myself to set the whole world on fire

H. I. Mavioglu

While witnessing my soul vanish into thin air?
Shall I run my business to benefit my life
And to choose my neighbor before I choose my ground?

When the winds of winter whistle over the ground
Pores of the earth are sealed up by crystallized water.
Is being anchored enough for the tree of life
If there were no open channels and open space
For its roots to spread? And then comes the warming air
Of spring which is a favor from a distant fire.

Cosmic forces link the ground with the empty space,
And wandering water is urged to float on air.
When core of life grows cold, who can warm it by fire

One More Open Door

What is likely to happen has happened before.
Even for a down-and-out there is a way out
For every tomorrow brings one more open door.

We may know what is stored, but not what is in store.
We see the building's stones, but not its binding grout.
What is likely to happen has happened before.

Growing overeager, we begin to explore
The uncharted paths of life and soon start to doubt,
Yet every tomorrow brings one more open door.

When expected stirring, spring showers start to pour,
Not only hemlock but also healing herbs sprout.
What is likely to happen has happened before.

It may be the winner's day to boast of his score
Which will merely quicken underdog's dormant clout
For every tomorrow brings one more open door.

There is a time to listen, a time to ignore
The background noise, and a time to stand up and shout.
What is likely to happen has happened before
And every tomorrow brings one more open door.

World of Dreams

He waived his dreams, probed his plans in detail,
Found them to be sound. He bypassed the trail,
Took the highway; initially drove slow;
Soon was driven with fears that he might fail.

Next he nursed a project in embryo
With latent power to evolve and grow;
For man and his endeavors will respond
To change, but nothing thrives in status quo.

Moreover, he formed a cohesive bond
With essence of nature to reach beyond
Its outer shell. Parts occupy their place,
But darkness hides the contents of a pond.

At last, he took the path to inner space
To find a chamber in his heart for Thrace;
Circulate Mount Ida in his blood stream
And put the Earth on his lap to embrace.

The world of illusions has a fixed scheme.
It scatters clues while hiding the supreme.
One may envision what's behind the veil
By taking refuge in the world of dream.

Naked Nature

To bloom once more, rose follows protocol,
But weather starts to play another number
With sheets of killing frost at early fall;
Later on, come the signs of Indian Summer.

First lions stalk the grazing wildebeest
Without a purr; tendons are tuned to glide
Over the savanna to kill and feast;
As they rest, come the rumbling roars of pride.

The epicenter of large earthquake strikes
With purpose to ruin everything en bloc;
As people pacify surviving tykes,
Comes the feeble tremble of aftershock.

What's fair? First lightning strikes and puts me under.
As I'm charred, comes the warning sound of thunder.

The Gift

I

A cut gem can be kept as a keepsake,
But feelings can't be wrapped and put aside.
The gift is warmth passing through a handshake;
Hence one's warm feelings are intensified.

II

My grandfather gave me a spinning top.
At his death, I spent my share of his land.
Still the top of my childhood spins nonstop
For it's powered by the warmth of his hand.

III

Clad in thorns, rose weathers the coldest day
To learn when to bloom and when to withstand.
The gift is not to give and show the way,
But it's passing the passion through the hand.

IV

While we were being controlled by the reign
Of tangled feelings, we twined and untwined.
Still the gift perseveres since I retain
The echoes of your voice within my mind.

V

Long-term bonds last no longer than a space.
Seize the fleeting moment and hold on fast.

A Couple Of Words

The gift is the clear mirror of your face
On which I see the image of our past

VI

Now plunge into your inner space and let
Yourself see how from One all had begun.
The gift and the blessing is to forget
Being "You" and "I" and become one.

VII

To take the path toward enlightenment,
We must cast off the weight of worldly needs.
On judgment day, a gift we must present.
The only proper gift is our good deeds.

Masked Blessings

I

She's unaware of my existence.
Still I feel I'm under her grips.
I relax and let the air bridge
The gap between our lips.

II

When the rose opens her lubricous
Lips for everyone to see,
She's trying to charm a bee without
Hiding her beauty from me.

III

When I am feeling blue and buried
In the darkness of night,
Above the other half of Earth,
The sun is shining bright.

IV

By the time I ascend foothills,
My joints begin to creak,
They're healed as I cheer a man who's
Descending from the peak.

V

I pause and pick out a book of
Poetry from the shelf

A Couple Of Words

And cherish the poems as if
I've written them myself.

VI

When the Prince of Darkness makes me
Feel, as though, I'm less blessed,
I say, "God has purpose beyond
My selfish interest."

Imperceptible Time

Since my retirement, I've been inching through a maze.
Ah. Yes. One day a week I fish, one day I dote
On grandkids but can't account for the other days.
Though, I keep time as the rhythmic waves rock my boat.

I've littered my trail with lost loves' cinders and ashes.
Since I've no time to act, shall I ignore their flashes?

Identity

I

"A shapeless life is my fate," said the Clay.
"I absorb the moisture to spread and swell;
Then I shrink and crack under the sun's ray.
Through rhythms, I bring forth the living cell.

"To acquire a shape, I pass through the blaze,
Thus my soul is sealed by the outer glaze."

II

The Rock, "It is my lot to have a shape.
I may look firm and lasting in my prime
Though the brunt of forces I can't escape.
I'm the soft grain for the gristmill of time.

"I shall lose my shape but shall not dismay.
I'm the son of Fire and the source of Clay."

III

"I have none of my own and yet I take
Any shape." said the Water. "I'm a brook,
Then an ocean, then the dew of daybreak,
And the colorless ink of the First Book.

"Having no shape or color is my prize.
I fill the well of life of any size."

IV

The Air, "I can't tip the scale with my weight.
Still I bear the weight of a bird on wings.
By being void of shape, I penetrate
Deep into the cells of all living things.

"I start life on breath, and I never wean.
I'm for life without being touched or seen."

V

The Fire, "I don't consume; I purify
Everything I touch. Also I maintain
The warm furnace of life. When my supply
Is exhausted, the darkness starts its reign.

"To forge the cosmos, He devised a force
By utilizing me as His resource."

VI

The Life Force, "I'm the mysterious power
Behind the chicken and egg…grass and seed.
For each living thing there's a final hour,
But my constant presence is guaranteed.

"The life weighs much more than its aggregate
For the life's parts weigh less than the life's weight."

VII

A Trailing Plant, "I clothe the naked grounds
And hold the cancer curing alkaloid.
I am called the dogbane and sprayed by hounds,
But I am neither honored nor annoyed.

"When my flowers fade, no one cares to sprinkle.
Yet my sap proves that I'm the Periwinkle."

A Couple Of Words

VIII

The Wolf, "I rely on my close-knit team,
Not on my fangs. I spook the herd, then pull
Back to see which one will run out of steam
While watching for the sharp horns of the bull.

"I prey on the flaws of old age and youth,
But in the scheme of things I'm a blunt tooth."

IX

The Bread, "I harvest live grains and amass
To go through the mill, through the eyes of a sieve
To turn shapeless. I rise and fall, then pass
The test of an oven to grow nutritive.

"As folks give grace, I feel blessed for I'm able
To sustain life. May I honor your table?"

X

The Backgammon Board, "I've seen games of skill;
Also I've witnessed the bias of dice.
With a mere ambsace, one might rush to kill
His foe's men where a master would think twice.

"Your opponent may be skillful and faster;
Still, with a good throw, you can beat the master."

XI

When a staunch one who came through an ordeal
Comes to my attention, I am not quite
Ready or willing to affix the seal
Of success, unless I feel his insight.

I know the man—the way he might appeal
To reasoning and the way he might feel.

XII

I'll never see through the deep-seated fears
Of a man whom I believe to be brave.
I'll never know if one's up to his ears
In intrigues, though he looks refined and grave.

Since the inner man I can't penetrate,
Shall I then judge him by his outward fate?

XIII

By hard work, I grew into a tycoon
And kept pushing, for I am an upheaver.
Then I witnessed that the riches were soon
Blown by the fate; since then I'm a believer.

Not that I believe, but what I believe.
Not that I achieve, but how I achieve.

XIV

I said, "Nowadays folks are growing rude.
A neighbor is turning against his neighbor.
They are developing an attitude
That one can live on someone else's labor."

A voice said, "Judge as kindly as you can.
The mirror of man is another man."

XV

I sought to know man's true identity,
He hid it from me with a veil of smiles.
After a long friendship, he let me see
Not his life as it is, but his life styles.

Men have no right to understand their lives.
Their files are kept secret in God's archives.

Retiring on the Job

We no longer classify men as the citizens and the slaves.
Now we have the elite and the mob.
Marauders are gone; now we have the glut of knaves
And they fleece us by retiring on the job.

Is There a Defect in the Design?

Has the peak of the mountain grown too proud
And conceited by breathing the thin air?
Where are the tall trees? Are they not allowed
There or did they flee and left the peak bare?

A peak must toil behind the mist to milk
The moisture from the drained clouds as they pass,
And it must guide the liquid thread of silk
To reach where the pine seeds sprout thick like grass.

Which one of those seedlings shall be a tree
By undergoing real world's ordeal?
Shall it decipher its own mystery
Of staying power? Than shall it reveal?

Deep in the woods, a doe was lying next
To her aborted double headed fetus.
She asked to herself, for she was perplexed,
"Without a start, why some meet their quietus?"

From their land, folks wished to purge the conflicts.
Their welfare pools were all ready to flood;
Still the streets were owned by the derelicts.
For one can't get a rose from every bud.

If something is crooked, don't rush to straighten
Unless you know why God created Satan.

Straight Lines Curve

Every straight highway has a way to curve.
Even the simplest words have overtones.
While telling the truth, people never swerve,
But the tongue can slip for it has no bones.

Say whatever you want to say; don't halt.
Regardless of what you say, they find fault.

Crimson Poppy

I

As if it were an eggshell, she cracked the crust
Of the Earth and freed
Herself but felt lost under the dome.
At once, she started to comb
Her new world, found nothing lacking, but she was in need
Of time to adjust.

II

Devoted Mother Earth was still holding her
By her flimsy root.
Since she was not utterly alone,
Rejected, cut off and thrown
Into a hostile world, she felt safe, and nature's brute
Force looked kindlier.

III

She was still dazed, all naked and monochrome,
Yet her tiny pores
Opened to breathe, and her chlorophyll
Photosynthesized with skill.
She was then convinced that life was opening its doors
To welcome her home.

IV

"Only yesterday I was like a lost pup,"
Said a budding sprout.
"But life is leisurely over here,
When you're chilled by the night air,

A Couple Of Words

The next day you'll be warmed for Father Sun will come out.
You too will grow up."

V

Being located over a sandy loam,
She had room to cast
Her rootlets after the moisture in
The soil and unfurled her thin
Leaves to store the Sun's power, and she burst forth
As the downy brome.

VI

She built a fine figure to become the belle
Of the open field.
Her veins were distended with rich milk;
Her blond hair was soft as silk.
Among ordinary ones as well as the well-heeled
She was nonpareil.

VII

Soon she balked, "This is my life. Why should I spend
It in a retreat?
I refuse a luxurious life fraught
With greed, and I won't be caught
In the web of loneliness for life is incomplete
Without a close friend."

VIII

She noticed other sprouts and leaned toward them
And whispered, "Hello,
My name is Crimson Poppy. I'd like
To be your friend." "I am Mike,"
Replied a handsome sprout. She turned red and felt a flow
Of warmth in her stem.

IX

A seer read her leaves, "Your mother is a green
Thumb, and you will be
The one to dethrone the Asphodel;
All will fall under your spell.
In the Elysian Fields, you will live in harmony
And rule as the queen."

X

Crimson thought, "I neither can defame a seer
Nor can I be naïve.
I cannot see beyond the next mound
For I'm just above the ground.
It's not the time to be distrustful or to believe
Everything I hear."

XI

Sprouts were rooted; no one was a newcomer.
They were building more
Self-confidence by the end of spring.
Thereon, they were channeling
Their reserve energies toward the final show for
It was midsummer.

XII

Then it was the season for poppies to bloom.
They were giving their
Best but their skills were short on detail,
And the petals were too pale.
Yet they were well pleased, knowing that what else they might bare
The soil would consume.

XIII

She was told, "Forget the Seer and infantile
Dreams and do your deed."
She replied, "I'll fill every bower
With a rare crimson flower

A Couple Of Words

To create such an original artwork, one must proceed
With a refined style."

XIV

The Sun was approaching its zenith with zeal
Believe me Mister,
It was staying there day after day
Just like a monster x-ray
Machine installed above the Earth to burn and blister,
Not to help or heal.

XV

Hot and long days gave her a weird sensation,
More like journeying
Through the most beautiful land of dreams.
There were green fields and cool streams.
She could not imagine it, but she was suffering
From dehydration.

XVI

Her rootlets were clinging to the Earth's dry breast.
Earth, "Don't misconstrue,
I'm not what you think I am, Daughter.
I do not create water.
It comes down from clouds, and when that happens, I'll give you
All you can ingest."

XVII

And Cloud said, "I'm a powerless vagabond
Who is forced to race
Toward some godforsaken parched land.
I must bow to the command,
But when the forces allow me, I'll form at your place
A seasonal pond."

XVIII

Sun said, "I've forgotten how to close or blink
My eyes long ago.
I can't tell what's the day? What's the night?
I may look knowing and bright,
But I've no choice for on the chain of Cosmos I'm no
More than a weak link."

XIX

Her flesh seared but her soul began to ascend
From the scorching pot
Of Earth, then floated above the Sun
And united with the One.
At last life came full circle. The Soul rode the chariot
Of time without end.

XX

During her journey, she stopped at Paradise
Where streets were inlaid
With fine silver and sidewalks were gold,
Crimson silk rugs were unrolled
For the rite; she pondered about her fate, "What I paid
For was the right price."

XXI

The next spring came with a warm smile to entice
Seeds to germinate.
As young poppies thrived with their playmates,
Crimson watched them from the gates
Of Heaven and said, "I sought no guidance, and I hate
To proffer advice."

The Rose and the Weed

I

Behind the iron gates of the garden, the Rose
Seems to be happy. In her weeded bed she sips
Spirits to suppress deep fears that only she knows.
While watching gardener, she dares not to open her lips,
Knowing she'll be grabbed by the neck and sold for profit
And by careless lovers be treated as a snippet.

II

Beyond the garden, on the cliffs, I found a place
Where I neither bow to gardener nor beg for rain.
I hold the secret of extracting sap from trace
Of moisture in the soil, sufficient to sustain
Constant ticking of my biological clock.
I am the Weed: I thrive in the crack of the rock!

Emmanuel

During their late afternoon rounds, the nurse
And physician entered the patient's room.
There, the ladies from San Xavier Church
Were forming a tight ring around the bed
And reading aloud from the Spanish Bible
And the prayer books. The physician did
Not comprehend the recital, and yet
The mystical aura was mesmerizing.

The tone would start mournfully. One might guess,
The reading is about no other valley
Than "The Valley of the Shadow of Death."
Then the sound would get softer. One might feel,
They're alluring the Savior of the Soul.
Abruptly, the pitch would get loud, then louder;
Shrill, then shriller. One might surmise, they're trying
To drive away the Snatcher of the Soul.
Then it would grow triumphant. One might think,
They're celebrating the Eternal Life.

The doctor shook off the spell, without breaking
The rhythm of reading, advanced nearer
The bed to re-examine the patient.
He passed his hands through a gap between two
Portly ladies.

        The patient's chest felt like
A field, furrowed and then forgotten, sunken
Over the intercostal spaces, ridged
By the ribs, parched by the hot summer sun.

A Couple Of Words

On that windless surface nothing was stirring.
Through his stethoscope, he could hardly hear
The muffled sounds of life echoing in
A hollow chest. This was the time to wait.

After doing everything humanly
Possible, doctors can't wait patiently.
People say, "Physicians love to play God."
But, in fact, they act like the common folks.
Since men lack the virtue of being patient,
Physicians are also impatient players
In a medicine show. They display their
Tools and remedies to the audience,
But no mortal is the Keeper of life.

Even Job was tested for his firm faith,
Not for his patience. He passed the test by
Keeping his faith in God. Since Job believed
In his innocence, he impatiently
Asked for the meaning of his suffering.

Only God chooses to harbor no needs.
He lays His laws down beyond eternity,
And patiently waits to let His will happen.

The doctor and nurse read each other's thoughts;
And they left the patient's room silently.
The words resounded in the doctor's mind:
"Jesus, Dios, Espiritu Santo-"
Somehow he grasped the meaning of the words.
If one were to master the meaning of
"Jesus, Dios, Espiritu Santo-"
Is there anything else to understand?

As the physician arrived in his office,
Father Garcia paid a hasty visit
To ask about the patient's prognosis;
Though he ignored what the doctor might say.
Also he did not care if anyone

H. I. Mavioglu

Were attentive to what he himself had
To say.

      Not to demand compliancy
From the doctor, the priest fixed his keen eyes
On the diplomas and certificates
Decorating the wall behind the desk.
For the priest, those papers meant nothing more
Than the dry leaves, pressed between the pages
Of an old book. Their usefulness was to
Remind the collector of seasons past.
The priest began to talk softly, as if
To himself.

      "All through his life, Emmanuel
Worked everyday from sun up to sun down,
On the flat plains and in the sunken valleys.
He was the picker of the Earth's bounties.
He lived closer to the soil and the dust.
He was like fine-grained clay, packed down, layered,
Then molded and shaped, not by the hands but
With the weight of the world, baked by the sun,
Polished smooth by the blowing winds and sands,
Bathed clean by the cleansing heavenly showers.
Season after season, year after year.

"His working year would begin at the orange
Groves of Florida and come to an end
At the apple orchards of Washington.
He left a zigzag path across the plains
And the valleys. He cataloged and stored
Their dust in his lungs and their pesticides
In his inner organs to prove the point.
He worked them all; whether well-known or not:
Rio Grande, Imperial, San Joaquin,
Sacramento, Willamette, Yakima,
And Wenatchee.

A Couple Of Words

"Last fall, for the first time,
He could not finish the Wenatchee picking.
I knew then that was the end of the road,
Both for him and for his pickup camper.
His hands were good at picking ripened fruits,
But they never picked a single welfare
Or unemployment check.

"I told him that
He could have been harvesting his social
Security checks for so many years.
I'd help him to file applications to claim
His benefit and find him a place to live.
He was not feeling that puny, he said;
Maybe a little tired, or growing old
Or getting lazy like other folks.
Though he'd seen ripened fruits fall with the pull
Of their own weight during a windless night,
He was returning to South Florida.
There with the warm sun, his joints might loosen.

"During his younger years, when his friends would
Ask, 'Emmanuel when are you going
To get weary of wandering around?
Do you ever think about settling down?
He felt accused of doing something wrong.
As if he had to answer, he'd reply:
'I'm planning; I'll purchase a patch of land
In a valley to grow my own orchard.'

"As he picked, he watched and saw everything.
Robins and hummingbirds arrived in time
To celebrate the spring, and they escaped
Just before the cold winds began to blow.
Sparrows stayed in one place, fair or foul weather.
Their dissimilar lifestyles neither made
Sparrows virtuous nor did they make migrant
Birds vagrants.

H. I. Mavioglu

"Deeds to land changed hands as if
They were money. People talked about land
Division or merger, but on the land
Nothing changed except the sites of the stakes.
The color of the earth remained the same.
Trees continued to bloom and bear according
To demands of the seasons, not in step
With the whims of someone who held a piece
Of paper in his hands.

Emmanuel
Thought that deeds to the land were fraudulent;
For not a single one of them was signed
By the First Owner.

"Ever since he grew
Contented and pleased with his stage in life;
For he was the picker for the First Owner.

"Now, he neither has an aim to keep him
Going nor does he have too much to lose.

"He'll keep his weather-beaten rosary
Around his neck. He did not know what to
Do with his sad-eyed red clay crucifix.
By chance, that problem had its own solution;
Without any influence of distinct
And physical forces, it fell and shattered.
I picked up its fragments, so that not a
Chip of it might end up in a trash can.
This is a sign to remind Emmanuel
That Jesus would die again for his sins.

"He has no family that we know of.
He used to send money to somebody;
The money orders were returned years ago.
No hands were left to receive and prize them.

A Couple Of Words

"For years, he had no one to take care of,
And caring for himself was easy for
He had but few needs.

"He neither belonged
To my parish nor to any other.
He gave me cold cash to cover the cost.
We will be happy to lay him to rest.
He's acquainted with dust.

"Folks might think I judge
Them on the basis of their church attendance.
Actually I read the palms of their hands.
Emmanuel's palms are layered with calluses,
And torn by the thorns. A man of those palms
Could not have time to get into mischief.

"When the fire of loneliness got intense,
He used to sprinkle some tequila on them.
It is hoped that it mollified his pain."

A nurse called, "Doctor you should examine
The patient in room six-thirteen C."
This time, he heard nothing but stark silence.
He nodded to the nurse, sneaked out and shuffled
Toward his office, feeling exhausted.
His stethoscope felt like a noose around
His neck to choke him. How can a physician
Feel peaceful when he loses a patient?

The nurse pushed on the call button and asked
An aide to team up with her with a gurney.
She switched the bedside buttons to neutral,
Turned off the cardiac monitor, suction
Machine, respirator and the oxygen;
Put on a pair of gloves, pulled out the IV
Needles and dropped them into a sharp-box.
She pulled out the tubes from the orifices,
Placed them in a bag and sealed it.

H. I. Mavioglu

In time,
The aid arrived, and she started to work
By peeling the electrodes from the chest.
They took off the soiled gown, cleaned the body
And put on fresh pajamas.

While the joints
Were loose and muscles were supple, they closed
The jaw shut; straightened the leg and the arms;
Crossed the arms over the stomach and placed
The right hand over the left hand; pulled down
The upper eyelids to close the eyes; placed
A penny on each lid.

As the cold kettle
Is powerless to lift the lightest lid,
The blinkless eyes as well shall stay still under
The weight of a cent.

It was an old custom
To place silver quarters on the eyelids.
By using copper-clad zinc pennies, are
They apologizing to the deceased?
"Sorry fellow, although we took your life
Savings, we are not getting wealthy. See!
All we can spare is a couple of zinc cents."

They tagged the right great toe and placed the body
In a body bag and then zipped it closed,
Scribbled the name of the deceased on it,
Transferred the body bag with its content
To the gurney. They spread a sheet upon
The remains, letting the bed sheet hang loose.
All one could see was an eminence at
The middle of the gurney.

The aid took
The freight elevator down to the basement
To deposit the package at the morgue.

A Couple Of Words

Two lady housekeepers rolled in with carts.
One was loaded with deodorants, soaps,
Disinfectants, spray cans, mops, and buckets.
The other was piled high with linens.

They knew their routine. Without wasting time,
They took their daily small dose of gossip.
No career jargons were passed around
Like the ones used by the medical staff.
"Mostly saving lives, rarely losing one."

They'd cleaned these rooms several times before.
As one goes out, another one comes in.
As the ripples upon the sea of life
Exist at all by canceling each other.

They turned the TV and quickly found
Their favorite soap opera. As they listened,
One stripped the bed down to its plastic cover;
Rolled soiled sheets and stuffed them into the hamper.
She sprayed and wiped away the smeared covers;
Collected the faded flowers and crushed
Them to reduce their bulk down to a size
To fit the trash can; gleaned the get-well cards.
The full thickness of the cards neither stretched
The distance between her index finger
And thumb nor took much room in the wastebasket.
She sponged the table and the bedside stand;
Made the bed; slipped pillowcase on the pillows,
And fluffed them up; spread a blanket on
The bed and finished her share of the work.
The other lady mopped the floor; removed
The stains from the walls. She poured chemicals
Into the toiled bowl; then brushed and flushed;
Finally, sprayed the room with deodorizers.

Before leaving, she fogged the evidence.
Yet the hospital smell was lingering.

H. I. Mavioglu

The room was groomed for the next guest to rest,
But for the span of a wink of an eye.

Shades of Change

I

Technology emblazons its plastic skin, steel
Skeleton and microchip brain. They can scrub smoke,
Yet let its ghost harm like radiation and feel
That what is concealed cannot hurt the common folk.

With new skyscrapers we might as well be impressed
Since hunchbacked old temples are too tired to contest.

II

He went back home in search of a familiar site,
Past the faceless hazy city, this side of green
Fields, he said, "Now, I remember this place; "In spite
Of gray moss on the stones, dates 'from-to' could be seen.

A few were upright, but the rest were lying down.
"God is Eternal" was carved on their crumbling crown.

Beauty Remembered

I

The sun said, "For eons I've been
Laboring day and night.
Today I'll play and bless all with
Optimum warmth and light.

"I'll send down not my fire but my
Rays brighter than before.
Green grapes require more heat to ripen
But that's tomorrow's chore."

II

The sun's golden rays turned the weather
Balmy in a short while,
And the living things expressed their
Gratefulness with a smile.

The sunshine was brightening colors
In many pleasing ways.
On the mirror of bays, sunrays
Were dancing with sunrays.

Serene peace and tranquility
Were ruling everywhere.
The ocean was blessing the land
With a fresh breath of air.

A Couple Of Words

III

Feast your eyes on sunshine, palm trees
And the waves of the seas.
Full life is not a passing storm
But it's a lasting breeze.

IV

An old couple cherished the day.
As they walked hand in hand
On the beach, their hearts throbbed and their
Blood stirred by the warm sand.

They were not merely spectators
But participants of
The beach scene for they were acquainted
With all the ways of love.

Once each one of them would confront
The challenges headlong.
Then love made them weak but their twined
Weaknesses made them strong.

V

They passed by the beach crowd for those
Young people had no plans
Save to flaunt their physique and to
Deepen their golden tans.

VI

The flowers in the garden of
A villa on the beach
Front were blooming and boasting their
Colors from blue to peach.

In that grand garden, a girl was
Reading with dreamy eyes.
She was too innocent to have
Said too many good-byes.

She closed the book and stepped down to
The beach to take a short
Amble by herself without a
Boyfriend or an escort.

The Couple viewed her with adoring
Eyes, but not to distract
Her, they gave not a smile nor did
They make an eye contact.

VII

She was not wearing a swimsuit,
Instead a dapper dress.
She looked so regal that the Couple
Nicknamed her 'The Princess.'

For her figure her see-through dress
Was a fitting outfit.
In a bikini she could not
Have looked more delicate.

The dress was hugging her warm body.
Waves were kissing her knees.
And with her body language, she
Was airing her heartsease.

Her steps were so measured as if
She were on a high wire.
With her fine frame she would have looked
Fair in any attire.

Her form rippled with graceful muscles;
Her eyes mirrored the blue
Of calm seas, and her head was balanced
With a chignon hairdo.

VIII

While molding her face, God must have
Been pleased with His creation.

A Couple Of Words

And her bewitching eyes were leaving
Room for imagination.

IX

They had no facts about the Girl
But that did not deter
The Couple from composing a
Character sketch for her.

X

Wife said, "Our Princess is not a
Day older than sixteen,
And in her world of dreams, she is
A teenage beauty queen.

"In her springtime of life, her feelings
Are like a tangled skein.
Like a spring day, she can't decide
Whether to shine or rain.

"She is young although she does not
Appear to be naïve.
In time, our Princess will learn how
To give, how to receive."

XI

Man said, "Yes, she looks sensible.
And yet who can foresee
If she'll be granted gladness and
Love by the destiny.

"When a lover vows to love her
And still he goes away,
Would she sense that lovers are fickle,
But love does not betray.

When she matures and reaches to
Her prime, she will exude

Charms; what satisfies our eyes now
Is only a prelude.

"Bids go high for a purebred filly.
Still one is game to pay
The price with the hope that someday
She'll have a winning day.

"People's dormant desires rouse when
They see a waxing crescent
Knowing that under the full moon
Their nights grow opalescent.

"She has been searching for a way
 "Out of her labyrinth
 Of teens and holding her head high
 Like a green hyacinth.

"When a grown hyacinth falls in
Love with her flowering
Self, she bends to kiss the image
Reflecting in a spring."

XII

Princess passed by the boys and left
Them there without regret.
When a handsome youth appeared over
The beach ridge, their eyes met.

XIII

Wife said, "Nobody has been able
To write the 'how to' book
Of love but it starts in the lovers'
Eyes with a longing look.

"By playing a guessing game we've
Passed the time on the shore.
But it's odd when you act as if
You have known her before."

XIV

Man said, "That Girl's beauty and grace
Including her hairdo,
Isn't a déjà vu. I've known her
Since the day I met you."

Let's Bless Them All

Why peruse people? We know they falter and fall.
We perceive mortals' deeds but can see no one's soul.
Let's embrace the souls as they are and bless them all.

Some may appear to be having a nonstop ball,
Even the luxurious living takes its toll.
Why peruse people? We know they falter and fall.

Some may be rich yet they may be in their wealth's thrall;
Others may be free while they're living on the dole.
Let's embrace the souls as they are and bless them all.

Some lust to control others and like to stand tall;
Others know the only control is self-control.
Why peruse people? We know they falter and fall.

Surely, some sell their souls for drugs and alcohol,
While others give up life itself to reach their goal.
Let's embrace the souls as they are and bless them all.

A streetwalker flirts with johns that make her flesh crawl.
A monk meditates in his cozy cubbyhole.
Why peruse people? We know they falter and fall.
Let's embrace the souls as they are and bless them all.

Man Would Not Begin if he Were Afraid of the End

Life forms, by being split, hatched or born, need
To fill their space in line with nature's will.
Living things for eons carry the past
Genetic codes that force them to thrive now.
Then the same genes show the way to their end.
And all endings give meaning to the future.

Each meddling of mankind transforms the future;
Therefore people will find themselves in need.
And yet the life source will last to the end.
Who can conquer nature's will with men's will?
Even the fittest beasts can't survive now
For our fathers stole their space in the past.

Do we polish the pieces of the past
To cast a bright picture upon the future?
Are we mesmerized by youthfulness now?
Is life but an illusion? Do we need
To be scared of time? By being so, will
We gain an extra second at the end?

By false hopes do we gain a worthy end?
Healing art advanced in the recent past,
Yet death rate is "one per person" which will
Remain a constant in the distant future.
Men talk of 'the hereafter' for they need
Religion, though most faiths are nameless now.

'Forever' won't apply for 'here and now'.
The natural laws set the birth and the end.

H. I. Mavioglu

The man-made laws are just for the flock's need;
But those laws changed no man's fate in the past.
To save my soul right now and in the future,
I'll merge with the state of oneness-of-will.

The flesh is a cloak for the mind and will.
I'll always prize my mind, as I do now.
Let no one stall my journey to the future.
The quest of man has neither start nor end.
Just having life was ample for my past.
Yet to be born—Here's my space for your need.

Oneness-of-will melds my birth with my end.
I'm at peace now with my present, my past,
And my future; being whole, I've no need.

DESECRATION OF DARTFORD PEAK

I. A Sudden Change

1
Zeke climbed up to the Dartford Peak
With a well organized
Mind to seize the Peak's image just
Before it's pulverized.

2
Not through his eyes but through the eyes
Of his mind, he could see
What eminence it used to be
And what a wreck it'll be.

3
When his labored breathing normalized,
He searched for a clue but found
No valid reason for what was
Happening all around.

4
Through the woods a strip was clear-cut,
And the grass was adust.
The naked earth was prone to take
To the skies with a gust.

5
Bulldozers must have made an easy
Meal of the north wall of
The Little Spokane Canyon after
A few days of push and shove.

6
The loose loam slid down the bank to
Cause a man-made landslide.
With man's meddling, a beautiful
Land was unbeautified.

A Couple Of Words

7
When one sharpens his dozer's blades
And mercilessly thrusts
Them into the earth, her wounds ooze
Till they're covered with crusts.

8
Yellow skins of dozers were covered
With heavy dust and clay.
They rested as do sated wolves
After eating their prey.

9
The peak stood at the canyon's south wall.
She'd given all she could give
All through her life. Now drillers were turning
Her bones into a sieve.

10
Boulders were coated with a whitish
Dust, spurting from the drill
Holes, which made them look as if they
Were terminally ill.

11
Drillers did not want to see any
Survivor or escaper.
To have room for their charges, they
Stuffed the holes with tarpaper.

12
As the rapist would stuff the mouth
Of his victim to rape;
Drillers could not afford to leave
The boulders' mouths agape.

13
The Peak was covered with a phantom
And polka-dotted drape.
One felt as if one were treading
On an eerie landscape.

14
Through the Canyon only the echoes
Of screeching brakes were heard,
Nothing else: no rustling of leaves,
No singing of a bird.

A Couple Of Words

II. One Spark Can Kindle Many Flame

1
When Zeke, lifted his tired eyelids,
Faith was standing nearby.
He could read what was on her mind
From the depths of her sigh.

2
One may not understand or hear
The words, yet before long
He senses that the chanteuse is
Singing a mournful song.

3
He had known her well, yet did not
Care to know her life's scope,
For their daily trails crossed each other
Only on the Peak's slope.

4
They were solo singers. They could
Not perform a duet.
Yet, their individual songs
Gained new depths when they met.

5
Over the years, neither of them
Made any attempt to tether
The other but their deep love for
This Peak bound them together.

III. We Choose What Is Sacred for Us

1
Faith said, "Zeke, when I saw you walking
Slowly up the street, I
Knew what was on your mind and where
You were heading and why.

2
"I should have given space to deal
With feelings of your own,
Still I am here for I can't bury
My loved one all alone.

3
"Though she is cut off from her plains,
This Peak is not withdrawn.
She has room for the birds to hatch
And for the doe to fawn.

4
"After all that damage, she did
Not fully convalesce,
Still she bewitches the kids with
A touch of wilderness.

5
"I don't claim to be a Sherlock
And I am not for hire,
But I know the kids were here from
The ashes of their fire.

6
"When we're driven with greed from profit;
And we rob and ransack
Nature; what is lost will never
Be retrieved or brought back.

A Couple Of Words

7
"If we were to lift our hands to
Fell things that stand erect,
Would we not betray the words which
We call love and respect?

8
"On this Peak, I've howled with coyote
And chirped with chickadee.
These moss-covered granites and tall
Pines are sacred to me."

IV. River Runs Downward but Returns Upward

1
Not to observe these misdeeds which
Were directed to maim,
Zeke watched the River as it flowed,
Changed and yet stayed the same.

2
As the smaller circles expand,
Our inadequacy
Won't let us perceive their center
Or their outer boundary.

3
A straight line is flawed till it forms
A ring with its other end.
A circle is a whole, for each
Dot aligns with its friend.

4
After their birth, streams run away
From the peaks to undergo
Changes to fly back to their birth
Peaks as rainfall or snow.

5
I know the nature of great rivers.
As they rush through a town,
They demand respect for they have
The potential to drown.

6
We can tame a great river to
Use it as a workhorse,
But it will tear down and run over
Everything in due course.

A Couple Of Words

7
Come spring runoff, the Spokane River
Would tumble down the falls
And the swollen waters batter
The shores like wrecking balls.

8
As I watch the pulsating stream
Of liquid energy,
I'd say, "This is the pulse of earth
Until eternity."

9
Come hot summer days, it, no longer
Being nourished and fed
By the snow, turns into a rippling
Sheet on its basalt bed.

10
When the desperate ones jump into
The Spokane River's waters,
It hides their secret past and corpses
Even from their own daughters.

11
A killer dumps the still warm body
While her jugular veins
Bleed into the Spokane River,
And it hides her remains.

12
Being challenged by a great River,
Some kids make it their goal
To conquer it. Each time they cross,
The River takes his toll.

13
The Little Spokane does not flow
Just to baptize and bless

The land, but also exemplifies
What it means cleanliness.

14
Cooks and Saddle Mountains store up
The drops to deliver
Them to the surface at the head
Waters of the River.

15
As it meanders, it gleans spring
Fed creeks, not to gain power
To submerge and drown the towns but
To nurture a frail flower.

16
Among its peers, the Dragoon Creek
Is a true entrancer;
By harboring small fish, it lures
The hooded merganser.

17
Between the River and its shores,
There is good chemistry.
Since each keeps itself clean, the River
Maintains its purity.

18
Its West Branch runs through Diamond Lake,
Then dips into Sacheen
And other lakes before it finds
Its twin in a ravine.

19
At any season, this calm River
Is always even tempered;
In its trusted bosom, children
Are entertained and pampered.

A Couple Of Words

20
With the spring thaw, the Little Spokane
River seldom rampages
Or shrinks under the summer sun
But stays calm through the ages.

21
Little ones, like the Little Spokane,
Provide a habitat
For the little creatures, but with
Strong foes they can't combat.

22
Either we're satisfied that it
Can provide swimming holes
For the young ones or pump it dry
To flush our toilet bowls.

V. Zeke's Memories Reshape What Is Shapeless

1
On the endless tape of time, men's
Time's but a narrow band.
And my days are too swift to be
Clocked by the second hand.

2
Yet during my days, we served not
As a custodian,
But squeezed the life from the Canyon
Of the Little Spokane.

3
I remember when Ravilla
Was the River's flood plain.
Then we lacked the power to push
Hard against nature's grain.

4
Every fishing season, Spokane
Indians would frequent
The banks. The gap was slim between
The poor and affluent.

5
Salmon would run thick; we'd no need
For fishing lines or corks.
Spokanes caught them with their bare hands;
We tossed them out with pitchforks.

6
With the dawn of the Dam Age, salmon
Have disappeared throughout
The River. Now one longs to catch
A tiny rainbow trout.

A Couple Of Words

7
Since the salmon's disappearance, they've
Been enriching the banks
Of the River. Do I care for
More enrichments? No thanks.

8
The Peak was not just baptized by
Fire but she was forged through
Fire and reshaped by natural
Blows to be born anew.

9
This Peak used to rejuvenate
Herself with each daybreak.
She was in touch with her wetlands
And streams that fed her lake.

10
Beginning at the green flatland,
The Peak slowly would raise
Her head to observe the meadows,
Which grow fresh grass to graze.

11
Then came the age of explosives,
Diamond drills and the dozer.
These pushed the peak toward her fate
Ever closer and closer.

12
The Peak had withstood glaciers,
But she could not survive
The firm assaults made by U.S.
Highway three-ninety-five.

13
When the crew came with explosives,
She had no place to hide.

After a short stand, she lost her
Entire eastern hillside.

14
Her eastern plain and lake became
Two waifs after the quake.
For the highway came between them
Like a smooth skinned black snake.

15
The Waifs were named; Meadow Wonder
And Mere Wonder. These dear
Ones were claimed by some folks who changed
Their names to Wandermere.

16
Meadow Wonder was treated as
A potential resource;
She was dressed in green furs and groomed
To become a golf course.

17
In green velvety clothes, she no
Longer looked meadowy
And learned the art of pleasing her
Honored guests gracefully.

18
Mere Wonder was a friendly lake.
Since he harbored pondweeds
And mingled with marsh, they said, "Here's
Where the mosquito breeds."

19
The walls rose around him to dry
The marsh and kill the reed,
And they seeded the reclaimed grounds
With golf-course-grade grass seed.

A Couple Of Words

20
Now the lake is free from pesky life.
"Toxic wastes keep him clear,
Which seep from dumps," they say, but you
Can't believe what you hear.

Photography by
Karen C. Meyer

21
Taming the meadow and the lake
Was their initial plan.
The Peak was to be sacrificed
As the most prized corban.

22
They used to fatten the young ram
Before they'd sacrifice.
Now the sacrificial ram's cut
To pieces, slice by slice.

23
They blew the western hillside and
Cleared the rocks with cat's blade
To reduce the incline of Mill
Street to nine percent grade.

24
To straighten out the Dartford Drive,
They cleaved Peak's northern tip.
Those drill tracks remain on the cliffs
To flaunt their workmanship.

25
The southern tip has been hauled out.
Now anyone could fit
Another peak into the crater
Of the spent gravel pit.

26
All cut off, The Peak was there at
The mercy of the foe;

A Couple Of Words

And the foe has set a firm date
For the final deathblow.

27
One day, next to the old highway,
They began to build new lanes.
Don't question where they are going.
No one knows; no one explains.

28
The plan for a new high bridge next
To the old one was addressed.
Among other choices, they've chosen
A path straight through the crest.

Photography by
Karen C. Meyer

VI. The Bigger the Project, the Larger the Profit

1
Why build things through the beaten paths?
Cut through the craggy cliffs,
Fill in the gullies and provide
Jobs for the working stiffs.

2
Since you spend the all mighty dollar,
By all rights, you must win:
The bigger the project, the larger
The net profit margin.

3
To make money, you must spend money.
Buy explosives and buy
Supplies; let others have some crumbs
While you wolf the whole pie.

VII. Is There Anybody Who Cares?

1
Faith said, "Zeke, you may be condoning
All this subconsciously.
The new highway will raise the value
Of your landlocked property."

2
Zeke, "We can't entrust the land's safety
To one man's righteousness.
Trust must be squarely based upon
The common consciousness.

3
"How could ancient trees dodge lightning
And winds? It puzzles me.
Then I say, 'Their guardian angels
Must shield them carefully.'

4
"I have had enough strength to lift
My ax with energy,
But never had the strength to wield
Its power onto a tree.

5
"As I walk among my old trees,
I regard them with awe;
For I see my end when the mighty
One's cut down by a saw.

6
"Plundering of the land begins
By building a highway.
Once the gate is wide open, looting
Can wait for the next day.

7
"As the hungry puppies run after
The nursing bitch,
Contractors follow the roads to
Groom the land for the rich.

8
"First they devise an attractive
Name, such as Dartford Heights,
Then promise to provide country
Living for urbanites.

9
"Once the million-dollar homes are
Constructed, they will drive
The taxes so high that they'll eat
The landowners alive.

10
"I may keep paying my taxes,
And still my land will not
Be safe for it will be regarded
As an untamed wild spot.

11
"For the new suburb, my land will
Become a new neighborhood's
Unsolved problem. They will resent
Driving around my woods.

12
"Soon they will condemn that last piece
Of land so that they could
Connect the roads. They'll say, 'It's for
The good of the neighborhood.'

13
"When the roads crisscross my wild land,
Then each remaining piece

A Couple Of Words

Will be worth more. The bottom line of
The ledger will increase.

14
"See, how your worthless land will fetch
Lots of money," they'd tell.
But the things I'd buy won't be worth
One half the land I'd sell.

15
"The fate of the peaks is the same.
First, the roads take their share;
Then the rest will be cleared without
Leaving a nest or lair.

16
"Then they will be terraced and tamed,
Sewer canals will be
Installed and they'll be ready for
A new community.

17
"Cul-de-sacs will sprout from the stems
Of streets like clover leaves.
Mansions will fill the stripped and leveled
Small lots from eaves to eaves."

VIII. Can We Have Progress Without its Consequences?

1
We do not merely feel good but
Also we live among
The breathing and living green things
Whether we're old or young.

2
We're taught not to speak through our brains
But through our wiggly tongues.
We harm the earth's lungs and then talk
Of the health of our lungs.

3
We cut the trees and denude any
Dry or wetlands or glen;
When we start to choke, we'd ask, "Where's
The source of oxygen?

4
First, we lure the vehicles with
Tanks full of gasoline.
When they clog highways and byways,
We beg for them to burn clean.

IX. We Do Things Differently Since We Are More Civilized

1
Without desecration, building
On a hill was the rule.
We can still see the Seven Hills
Of Rome and Istanbul.

2
Nowadays, methodically,
We will be plundering
And flaying the hills before we
Start to build anything.

3
On lofty heights, ancients felt they were
Nearer to their Deity.
They built their temples there to hear
The heaven's symphony.

4
The temple priestess would dance in
Ecstasy to enhance
Her powers to reveal the mortals'
Destinies in her trance.

5
Nowadays the heights are afforded
Only by the hotels.
They are built not to last but for
The flings of mademoiselles.

6
They'd have honeymoon suites not for
Innocent brides and grooms,
But mostly for the people who
Can pay well for the rooms.

X. Who Is to Blame?

1
Faith said, "We may mourn over each
And every broken boulder;
Blame everyone else, yet the shame
Still rests on our shoulder.

2
"We've quenched our thirst but not bothered
To ask, 'How fares the fountain?'
Much less to feel gratitude for
The distant snowy mountain.

3
"They've been blowing up peaks for years.
We don't see for we're dazed.
Do you believe that this Peak is
The first one to be razed?

4
"Throughout the history of mankind,
Not one legislature
Defined what specific act is
A crime against nature.

5
"One can maim or murder nature;
Feed on it like an ogress,
And be absolved of any crime
By saying, 'This is progress.'

6
"If one talks about nature, who
Will listen? Who has time?
This apathy must be considered
As a worst sin and crime.

A Couple Of Words

7
"As always, The Spokesman-Review
Has been ready to cite
And recycle yesterday's news.
Why write of the Peak's plight?

8
"The first time, it had a short piece
About a new high bridge
Across the Little Spokane which will
Span it from ridge to ridge.

9
"The second time, it was front page
News for folks were unable
To use their phones when one of those
Bulldozers nicked the cable.

10
"It never bothered to discuss
How dearly it will cost,
Not only in terms of money
But what'll be really lost.

11
"A journalist, if he does not
Want his business to fail,
Writes about what we want; all we want
Is trivial detail.

12
"Since we've been desensitized by
Much multimedia,
We now can't tell the love songs from
The epicedia.

13
"When we see a peak in China
Is blown with a megaton;

Should we feel sad about it or
Should we say, 'Job's well-done?'"

14
Zeke, "Faith, you don't know how to rally
For your cause; you're a loner,
And being a loner is fitting
Only for The First Owner.

15
"See those people on the golf course,
They are a social crew,
But grazing where the grass is green
Is not enough for you."

16
Faith said, "I wish I were a golfer:
I'd putt a round or two,
Then lead a guy to the clubhouse,
Drink and go to the loo.

17
"I'd chase balls with women whether
The skies were gray or blue.
I'd make some friends and some of them
Bound to be well-to-do.

18
"When a highway would daunt my golf
Course, my friends' help I'd seek,
And they'd order their men, 'Pull back
And blast the Dartford Peak.'

19
"A peak attracts no crowds to cheer
For her, no crowds to stand
Up for her. She lures the few sans
Making any demand.

A Couple Of Words

20
"I wouldn't go along with any
Environmentalist.
Each time they've aimed at the wrong target
And each time they have missed.

21
"They felt no pain when the west side
Of the peak was blown up.
When wetlands were stuffed with her rocks,
They felt like a sick pup.

22
"They forced the offenders to clean
The wetlands. Being skilled,
They saved the fetus but they watched
When the mother was killed."

23
Zeke said, "Rocky peaks may stand in
The way to spoil one's plan,
Yet a peakless place reminds me
Of a toothless old man.

24
"A peak is the tallest when she's born.
Yet, its toll time will take.
Billions of years hence, she will be
As flat as a pancake."

25
"So let them tear down the whole peak;
Even annihilate.
They'll be helping cosmic forces
Without changing her fate."

XI. Impermanence

1
In men's affairs, Zeke never sought
Any permanency,
Though he acquired through the peaks some
Faith in geography.

2
He used to tell his friends: Turn west
Where the river will meet
The Peak; no, you don't need a number
Or a name for the street.

3
Follow the south shore of the River
Until you'll see a streak
Of silver running to the River;
That is the Dartford Creek.

Photography by
Joyce E. Mavioglu

A Couple Of Words

4
There, turn right and travel due north
To get into the small
Canyon of Dartford Creek; and stay
Next to the eastern wall.

5
When you see a great monolith,
Turn into my driveway.
Don't rush; you are always welcome,
And tea is on the tray.

Photography by
Karen C. Meyer

6
Since the peaks grew fleeting, they, whether
It is daylight or dark,
Can't show the way. Henceforth, Zeke must
Seek a man-made landmark.

A Couple Of Words

XII. Walking Away From a Lost Shrine

1
The next day, blasted loose rocks were
Slowly shifting upon
The loose rocks. What was once standing
There was forever gone.

Photography by
    Joyce E. Mavioglu

2
They walked quietly over the dead
Granite burial ground.
The bonds that once thrived on the solid
Rocks could now be unbound.

3
They parted, knowing in their minds,
That they had to resign

To their loss. Yet they felt as two
Pilgrims who lost their shrine.

4
Zeke was muttering which was not
Meant to be for my ear,
But I could perceive what he was
Saying for I was near.

5
"Since we have the technology
To destroy and to bring
Down the peaks in the name of progress,
Must we wreck everything?"

0-595-34721-5

Lightning Source UK Ltd.
Milton Keynes UK
UKOW01f0258041116
286793UK00001B/239/P